MINUTES
WITH
JESUS

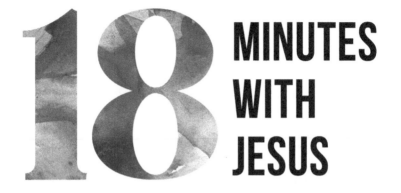

18 MINUTES WITH JESUS

STUDY GUIDE

Straight Talk from the Savior about
the Things That Matter Most

DR. ROBERT JEFFRESS

BakerBooks
a division of Baker Publishing Group
Grand Rapids, Michigan

© 2022 by Robert Jeffress

Published by Baker Books
a division of Baker Publishing Group
PO Box 6287, Grand Rapids, MI 49516-6287
www.bakerbooks.com

Printed in the United States of America

Library of Congress Cataloging-in-Publication Data
Names: Jeffress, Robert, 1955– author.
Title: 18 minutes with Jesus study guide : straight talk from the Savior about the things that matter most / Dr. Robert Jeffress.
Other titles: Eighteen minutes with Jesus
Description: Grand Rapids, MI : Baker Books, a division of Baker Publishing Group, [2022] | Includes bibliographical references.
Identifiers: LCCN 2021055596 | ISBN 9781540902429 (paperback) | ISBN 9781493437818 (ebook)
Subjects: LCSH: Sermon on the mount—Criticism, interpretation, etc.
Classification: LCC BT380.3 .J44 2022 | DDC 226.9/06—dc23/eng/20220120
LC record available at https://lccn.loc.gov/2021055596

Portions of this text have been adapted from *18 Minutes with Jesus* (Grand Rapids: Baker Books, 2022).

Published in association with Yates & Yates, www.yates2.com.

Baker Publishing Group publications use paper produced from sustainable forestry practices and post-consumer waste whenever possible.

23   24   25   26   27   28   7   6   5   4   3

When Jesus saw the crowds, He went up on the mountain; and after He sat down, His disciples came to Him. He opened His mouth and began to teach them.

Matthew 5:1–2

CONTENTS

INTRODUCTION AND TIPS FOR STUDY GROUPS

Before beginning your personal or group study of *18 Minutes with Jesus: Straight Talk from the Savior about the Things That Matter Most*, please take time to read these introductory comments.

If you are working through the study on your own, you may want to adapt certain sections (for example, the icebreakers) and record your responses to the questions in this study guide or, if preferred, a separate notebook. You might find it more enriching or motivating to study with a partner with whom you can share answers or insights.

If you are leading a group, you may want to ask group members to read one chapter from the *18 Minutes with Jesus* book and work through the corresponding questions in this study guide before each meeting. This isn't always easy for busy adults, so encourage group members with occasional phone calls, emails, or texts between meetings. Help group members manage their time by pointing out that they can cover a few pages each day. Also, encourage them to identify a regular time of the day or week they can devote to the study. They, too, may write their responses to the questions in this study guide or in a separate notebook.

Each session in this study guide includes the following features:

- **Session Topic**—a brief statement summarizing the session.
- **Icebreakers**—activities to help group members get better acquainted with the session topic and/or with one another.
- **Group Discovery Questions**—questions to encourage group participation or individual discovery.
- **Personal Application Questions**—an aid to applying the knowledge gained through study to personal living. (Note: these are important questions for group members to answer for themselves, even if they do not wish to discuss their responses in the meeting.)
- **Optional Activities**—supplemental applications that will enhance the study.
- **Prayer Focus**—suggestions for turning learning into prayer.
- **Assignment**—activities or preparation to complete prior to the next session.

Here are a few tips that can help you more effectively lead small group studies:

1. *Pray for each group member during the week.* Ask the Lord to help you create an open atmosphere where everyone will feel free to share with one another.
2. *Ensure each group member has the* 18 Minutes with Jesus *book and study guide.* Encourage each group member to bring his or her book, study guide, a pen or pencil, and a Bible to each session. This study is based on the New American Standard Bible (1995), but it is good to have several Bible translations on hand for purposes of comparison.

3. *Start and end on time.* This is especially important for the first meeting because it will set the pattern for the rest of the sessions.

4. *Begin each study session with prayer.* Ask the Holy Spirit to open hearts and minds and to give understanding so that truth will be applied.

5. *Involve everyone in the group discussion.* As learners, we retain some of what we hear and see, but we remember much more of what we hear, see, and do.

6. *Promote a relaxed environment.* If the group is meeting in person, arrange the chairs in a circle or semicircle. This allows eye contact among members and encourages dynamic discussion. Be relaxed in your attitude and manner, and be willing to share with the group.

one

Straight Talk about Your Happiness

SESSION TOPIC: Jesus began His talk by describing eight attitudes that will lead us to a joy-filled life. Matthew 5:3–12, a passage called the Beatitudes, includes some of the most familiar verses in the Bible, but they're also some of the most misunderstood. What does it really mean to be blessed? If we want to experience true and lasting joy, then we must grasp what Jesus meant when He said, "Blessed are . . ."

Icebreakers (Choose One)

1. What are some things that make you happy?

2. If you could choose to be either wealthy or happy, which would you choose and why?

Group Discovery Questions

1. What do you think it means to be "blessed"?

2. From what you read in this chapter, what is the difference between *happiness* and *joy*?

3. Why do you think it's difficult for Christians in our culture to be "poor in spirit" and approach God "in a spirit of utter dependence"?

4. Read Matthew 5:4 and 2 Corinthians 7:10. According to these verses, what benefits can result when we "mourn," or express sorrow over our sin?

5. Describe what you think Jesus meant to "hunger and thirst for righteousness" (Matt. 5:6). What would that spiritual hunger and thirst look like in everyday life? Be as specific as possible.

6. Read James 2:13. What are examples of situations in which mercy would be preferable to judgment? In Matthew 5:7, what did Jesus promise to those who show mercy?

7. The author said, "In Jesus's day, the Pharisees focused on their external appearance, wanting people to see their best side." Give examples of how we see this same attitude in today's society. In contrast, what do you think it means to be "pure in heart"? What blessing did Jesus give in Matthew 5:8?

Personal Application Questions

1. Have you ever longed for God's approval? How does it make you feel to know that the Beatitudes are the key to "God's approval and the lasting joy that accompanies it"?

2. Think of a time when you mourned the loss of a loved one, either through death or desertion. What did that grief feel like? Have you ever been sorrowful over your sin in a similar way? If so, what changes did you make in your life as a result?

3. What images come to mind when you hear the words *meek* and *gentle*? What did gentleness look like in the lives of Moses (Num. 12:3) and Jesus (Matt. 11:28–29)? In what specific ways can you show gentleness toward others?

4. Have you extended mercy to someone who wronged you, or has someone extended mercy to you? Describe what happened. What effect did mercy have in that situation?

5. Why is focusing on external behavior dangerous when it comes to your spiritual life? In what ways would your life be different if you were "pure in heart"?

6. Read Hebrews 12:14 and Ephesians 4:3. What are some things you can do this week to "pursue peace" in your life and the lives of others?

7. Have you ever been persecuted in some way for your faith in Jesus Christ? If so, describe what happened. What hope does Jesus's promise in Matthew 5:10–12 give you?

Optional Activities

1. Read James 2:15–16 and 1 John 3:17. What can your group do this week to extend mercy to someone in your church or community who is hurting or in need? Make a plan and follow through.

2. Make a list of the eight character traits mentioned in the Beatitudes. Beside each one, write an example of a practical way you can apply that trait to your life this week. For example: "*Mercy*—this week, when someone cuts me off in traffic, I will choose to extend mercy." Or "*Peacemaker*—this week, when I see a post on social media about a controversial subject, I will not spread conflict by posting a divisive comment."

Prayer Focus

Thank Jesus for giving us the Beatitudes, which provide the key to unlocking the blessed life. Ask God to help you develop these eight character traits. Confess the areas in which you fall short, and thank God for giving His approval and lasting joy to those who follow Him with a whole heart, adopting His attitudes and actions.

Assignment

1. This week, make the Beatitudes part of your everyday life by practicing one Beatitude each day. Meditate on that trait, and ask God to help you live it out throughout the day. If desired, journal about your experience and share with the group what you learned.

2. Read chapter 2 of the *18 Minutes with Jesus* book and work through the corresponding study.

two

Straight Talk about Your Faith

SESSION TOPIC: Christians are called to be salt and light—living out our faith in such a way that we cause others to thirst for God. The instructions on how to do that are found in the Word of God. It's a manual, so to speak, for living faithful and righteous lives. And since Jesus is the author of the Bible, we ought to understand what He thought about it and learn how to read it correctly (Matt. 5:13–20).

Icebreakers (Choose One)

1. Think of someone you know—or someone you've seen, such as a celebrity or pastor—who always seems to smile or have a joyful expression. How does this facial expression affect your perspective of him or her? Why do you think this person appears so joyful?

2. The author said, "How we live affects our witness to the world." Discuss examples—both positive and negative—of well-known Christians whose lives have affected their witness to the world.

Group Discovery Questions

1. What do you think our world would be like today if all believers stayed in their churches and "holy huddles" instead of mingling with people in the world?

2. As "the salt of the earth" (Matt. 5:13), believers are to live out our faith in such a way that we influence our world for good. Discuss examples of ways Christians today are making people thirsty for God.

3. In Matthew 5:13, Jesus warned about salt becoming "tasteless"—or, as the author put it, "so contaminated with the world it is impossible to differentiate between their lifestyle and the lifestyle of the average non-Christian." In what areas do you see Christians adopting the attitudes and actions of the culture around us? How does this affect Christianity's influence in our world?

4. Discuss the author's statement: "One of our functions as Christians here on earth is to stop the premature decay of society." In what ways do you see our culture decaying? How can believers today slow down this process of decay in our culture by how we live and what we do?

5. Read Matthew 5:16 and Philippians 2:15–16. Why do you think Jesus used the imagery of light in describing Christians? Which is more powerful: darkness or light? Discuss ways that our lives can be lights that attract those living in darkness.

6. Read Matthew 5:18. In a culture that is constantly changing its mind about what is acceptable and right, why is it important for us to bring our opinions about controversial subjects under the authority of God's Word?

7. According to Matthew 5:20, what kind of righteousness does Jesus require from us? Discuss what you learned in this chapter about how the scribes and Pharisees viewed external actions. Do you think Christians today tend to focus more on external actions or inner change? Which one do you focus on more in your own life?

Personal Application Questions

1. What do you think your face says about your faith right now? What, if anything, would you like to change about that?

2. Christians tend to go to one of two extremes when it comes to relating to the world: some Christians choose to isolate themselves from the culture, while other Christians choose to identify with the culture. Which of these views do you relate with more, and why?

3. Is the way you are living causing others to thirst after Christ? If not, what can you do this week to be more "salty" to unbelievers?

4. Are you stuck in the saltshaker? Do you spend all your time with other Christians? If so, what opportunities will you take this week to talk with unbelievers?

5. Do you tend to have a negative, fatalistic attitude about the dark culture in which we live, or do you tend to see this life as an opportunity to shine the light of Christ and spread the gospel? What changes can you make to your attitude this week, if needed?

6. Read 2 Timothy 3:16–17. To Jesus, all Scripture was equally authoritative and therefore equally important to obey and teach. Is there any biblical teaching that you are tempted to bend to conform to our culture? What did Jesus say about that?

7. In what ways are you engaging in "selective obedience" when it comes to God's standards? Confess any areas of disobedience to God and thank Him for His forgiveness.

Optional Activities

1. When we live our lives in wholehearted obedience to the Word of God, others will see our good works and glorify God. What can your group do this week to "put the spotlight on Christ"?

2. Look up profiles of famous Christians and discuss how they were "salt and light" to others. (Examples include William Wilberforce, Amy Carmichael, Hudson Taylor, Harriet Tubman, Billy Graham, Elisabeth Elliot, Fred Rogers, Dan Cathy, and Tim Tebow.) What can you do this week to emulate their example of being "salt and light" in your own community?

Prayer Focus

Thank God for giving us His Word, the absolute rule of faith and life. Confess to Him any ways you have compromised His Word or neglected to be "salt and light" in this world. Ask Him to help you live your faith in such a way that others will "see your good works, and glorify your Father who is in heaven" (Matt. 5:16).

Assignment

1. Is your workplace dark and bland? Is your school or your neighborhood filled with darkness and spiritual decay? This week, shine the light of Christ and add a little spiritual flavor to it. Be prepared to share your "salt and light" experiences with the group next week.

2. Read chapter 3 of the *18 Minutes with Jesus* book and work through the corresponding study.

three

Straight Talk about Your Relationships

SESSION TOPIC: When it comes to the subject of murder, we tend to think literally—about the physical taking of another's life. So did Jesus's original listeners. But Jesus meant more than the literal killing of another; He drove to the heart of the matter—hatred—and challenged us to examine our own hearts when anger gets the best of us (Matt. 5:21–26).

Icebreakers (Choose One)

1. Think of a leader who has a lot of power or influence, such as the president of the United States or a popular celebrity. How does that person's power and influence bring increased scrutiny and criticism? Would you like to be in that person's position? Why or why not?

2. Describe a movie or television show that demonstrates the destructive effects of anger and hatred.

Group Discovery Questions

1. True or false: "Sticks and stones may break my bones, but words will never hurt me." Explain your answer, offering specific examples if you can.

2. Read Proverbs 25:11 and Colossians 4:6. Why do you think the Bible stresses the importance of our words?

3. Read Matthew 7:28–29. How did the people respond to Jesus's teaching in the Sermon on the Mount? Why did they respond that way?

4. Read Matthew 5:21–22. What Old Testament command did Jesus quote in this passage? (See Exod. 20:13.) What did Jesus teach about this command?

5. What is the difference between sinful anger and righteous anger? Give an example of each.

6. If someone is not a Christian, does that give us the right to speak more harshly to that person? Explain your answer. What kinds of words do you think Christians should use when speaking with non-Christians?

7. Read Matthew 5:23–24 and 2 Corinthians 5:18–19. How do our personal relationships affect our worship of God? In what specific ways can Christians today carry out the "ministry of reconciliation" God has given us?

Personal Application Questions

1. Are you carrying around a crushed spirit from hurtful words spoken to you in the past? Read Jeremiah 31:3, Zephaniah 3:17, Psalm 34:5, Luke 12:6–7, and Ephesians 1:3–6 to find out what God says about you.

2. In Matthew 5:22, Jesus identified three ways we can be guilty of murder in our hearts: *anger*, *insults*, and *defamation* (harming someone's reputation). Which of these do you tend to struggle with more, and why?

3. Consider your activity on social media and other online forums. Could any of your posts or comments be considered angry, insulting, or defamatory? If so, confess your sin to

God and commit to honoring God with your words—spoken and written.

4. Do you tend to say things in anger or frustration that you don't literally mean? Or do you sometimes say something hurtful to someone and follow it with, "Just kidding"? Read Proverbs 12:18, Matthew 12:36, and Ephesians 4:29. What do you learn from those verses about how God wants you to speak?

5. Is there anyone who "has something against you" because you've hurt that person in some way, and you need to make amends (Matt. 5:23)? If so, what steps will you take this week to reconcile with that person?

6. When you get into an argument, are you usually the first to apologize, or do you tend to wait for the other person to apologize first? What are the benefits of being quick to apologize and ask forgiveness?

7. Read James 3:8–10. Think of a person you are holding a grudge against right now. Does the knowledge that the person is "made in the likeness of God" affect your attitude toward the person? What can you do to treat that person the same way Jesus has treated you?

Optional Activities

1. Break into groups of two or three. Share one situation in which you need to ask for forgiveness or seek reconciliation with someone. Commit to one concrete action toward reconciliation. Pray for one another.

2. Look up the words *reconcile/reconciliation* in a Bible concordance and read the verses you find. Choose one verse to memorize this week.

Prayer Focus

Thank God for "[reconciling] us to Himself through Christ" and giving us the "ministry of reconciliation" (2 Cor. 5:18–19). Confess any angry or hurtful words you have spoken and ask God to forgive you. Then ask Him to help you reach out to anyone you have offended and seek reconciliation.

Assignment

1. Write out the following two principles on a sticky note, and put it somewhere you will see it this week:
   * *Reconciliation is more powerful than revenge.*
   * *Reconciling today is wiser than reconciling tomorrow.*

2. Read chapter 4 of the *18 Minutes with Jesus* book and work through the corresponding study.

four

Straight Talk about
Your Sex Life

SESSION TOPIC: Like we do with murder, we tend to think of adultery in a literal sense: having sex with somebody who is not your spouse. But adultery doesn't begin in the bedroom; it begins in the heart and mind (Matt. 5:27–30). So we need to gain control of our minds before we lose control of our bodies, which too often leads to broken marriages. How can we do this? We can start by looking at what Jesus said about adultery (vv. 31–32).

Icebreakers (Choose One)

1. Think of a couple you know who have been happily married for many years. What are some specific things you admire about their marriage relationship?

2. Compare our society's view of adultery today with how adultery was viewed thirty years ago. In what ways have popular opinions about adultery changed? What reasons can you think of for this shift of perspective?

Group Discovery Questions

1. Read Matthew 5:27–28. What Old Testament command did Jesus quote in this passage? (See Exod. 20:14.) What did Jesus teach about this command?

2. Discuss the author's statement: "Adultery in the bed begins with adultery in the head." Do you agree or disagree? Explain your answer.

3. Read Genesis 1:28 and 1 Corinthians 7:3–5. What do these verses show us about God's perspective on sexual intimacy within marriage?

4. Have you, or someone you know, ever referred to someone as "eye candy" (or a similar phrase)? What are the dangers of labeling someone only by sexuality and physical appearance?

5. In Matthew 5:32 and 19:9, what serious offense did Jesus say provides biblical grounds for divorce and remarriage? Why do you think Jesus allowed for this?

6. Read 1 Corinthians 7:15. What is the only other situation in which divorce and remarriage are permitted? *Important note from the author: "If you are in an abusive marriage, then you are free under Scripture to get out of that house and protect yourself and your children. But if you end up divorcing because of abuse, the Bible says you must remain unmarried or return to your spouse (1 Cor. 7:10–11)."*

7. Read Genesis 1:27; 2:24 and Matthew 19:5. What do you learn from these verses about God's original design for marriage?

Personal Application Questions

1. The author said, "It's not merely a look that leads to sin; it's a certain kind of look, a lustful look. If we're not careful, looking can slip into lusting." Are you sometimes tempted to take a second or third look at someone in a lusting way? If so, what changes will you make to flee from this temptation?

2. Is sexual fantasy a sin if you don't act on it? Why or why not? (As you answer, consider Jesus's words in Matthew 5:28.)

3. Have you, or someone you know, been personally affected by divorce? If so, describe some of the lasting effects of divorce you or your loved ones have experienced.

4. Read Matthew 5:29–30. In this passage, how did Jesus (figuratively) describe how to deal with sin in your life? Why do you think He took such a severe approach to sexual temptation?

5. Are there any relationships or habits that are tempting you to think or act immorally? No matter how inconvenient or painful it may be, you need to deal decisively with that temptation right now. Confess it to the Lord and write out your commitment to "tear it out and throw it from you."

6. Read Proverbs 6:27. How does this proverb apply to sexual temptation in your life?

7. Have you committed sexual immorality, even in your heart? Read 1 John 1:9. The Bible says you can receive God's forgiveness. Admit that mistake to God and make the necessary changes in your life to honor Him in all your relationships from now on.

Optional Activities

1. *Develop a contract with your eyes.* Read Job 31:1. Follow Job's example and write a contract with your eyes. Consider specifying that you will never take a second, lustful look and that when speaking with somebody of the opposite sex, you won't have a wandering, lingering gaze. Also include any changes you will make regarding watching television and movies, reading books and magazines, and scrolling social media and the internet.

2. *Determine to think differently.* On a separate piece of paper, write Romans 12:2 and Philippians 4:8. Keep this paper in your Bible or put it near your television set or computer as a reminder that you can resist the pull to conform to sinful ways by choosing to transform your mind.

Prayer Focus

Thank God for His original design for marriage. Confess any sins of sexual immorality in your life. Ask Him to help you make the necessary changes to avoid sexual temptation and commit to honoring your mate (if you are married) and remaining pure in your thoughts and actions from this day forward.

Assignment

1. Memorize 1 Corinthians 6:18–20: "Flee immorality. Every other sin that a man commits is outside the body, but the immoral man sins against his own body. Or do you not know that your body is a temple of the Holy Spirit who is in you, whom you have from God, and that you are not your own? For you have been bought with a price: therefore glorify God in your body."

2. Read chapter 5 of the *18 Minutes with Jesus* book and work through the corresponding study.

five

Straight Talk about Your Adversaries

SESSION TOPIC: If we're honest, all of us have savored the thought of retaliating against someone who has hurt us. And in our age of social media, it's easy to get revenge by spreading lies and slander. Many of us have done just that. But Jesus offers a better way. Instead of seeking vengeance and holding grudges, let us learn to love and pray for those who've hurt us (Matt. 5:38–48).

Icebreakers (Choose One)

1. Think of a famous feud, such as the Hatfields and McCoys, the Capulets and Montagues (*Romeo and Juliet*), or the Jets and Sharks (*West Side Story*). What started the feud? What were some consequences of that feud?

2. Have you ever seen former adversaries become friends, either in real life or in a movie or television program? If so, describe what happened. What were the results?

Group Discovery Questions

1. Why do you think people want to seek revenge when they have been wronged? Discuss some consequences of our culture's philosophy of "Don't get mad. Get even."

2. Read Exodus 21:23–24. What do you think Moses meant by "eye for eye, tooth for tooth" (v. 24)? What boundaries did this Old Testament civil law provide to judges when pronouncing sentences in court?

3. Discuss the author's statement: "God never asks you to give up your right to justice. But as followers of Jesus Christ, when we are wronged, we are to release our desire for *retaliation*." Do you agree or disagree? Explain your answer.

4. Read Matthew 5:39. Does Jesus's command for believers to turn the other cheek mean we should not intervene in other people's conflicts? Why or why not? Use Scripture to support your answer (for example, Isa. 1:17; Ps. 82:3; Prov. 31:8–9). What does it mean for believers to "turn the other cheek" when personally wronged?

5. Read Matthew 5:42 and Luke 6:35. What are possible negative consequences of being generous with people? What are potential benefits of being generous?

6. Read Matthew 5:43–47. In what ways would our families, churches, neighborhoods, and nations be different today if we applied Jesus's teaching to "love your enemies and pray for those who persecute you"? What would obeying this command look like?

7. What do you think Jesus meant by "You are to be perfect, as your heavenly Father is perfect" (Matt. 5:48)? (See also Lev. 19:2.) Are believers able to be "perfect" (or "holy") in this life? Why or why not?

Personal Application Questions

1. Have you ever tried to get revenge? Or have you imagined ways to get back at somebody or thought of comebacks you wish you'd said at the time? If so, describe what happened. Why do you think you responded in that way? What was the result?

2. The law of *lex talionis*, applied personally, says if your spouse is messy, make a bigger mess to teach them a lesson. If your friend is late for lunch, make it a point to be later the next time. If a coworker makes a cutting remark out of frustration, blast that person on social media. Have you ever applied *lex talionis* to someone, or has someone responded to you in this way? Describe the situation. How did such a response affect your relationship?

3. In Matthew 5:39, Jesus said, "I say to you, do not resist an evil person." How do you typically respond to personal offenses? According to Jesus, how should you respond when you are personally wronged? What changes, if any, do you need to make to apply this teaching in your life?

4. Read Matthew 5:41. Have you ever gone the extra mile to help someone or done more than was expected of you? If so, what happened? In what ways does going the extra mile reflect the character and ministry of Jesus Christ?

5. In Matthew 5:42, Jesus said, "Give to him who asks of you, and do not turn away from him who wants to borrow from you." Describe a time when you were generous. What happened? What can you do to be generous with someone this week?

6. Read Matthew 5:43–44 and Luke 23:34. Why do you think Jesus taught and demonstrated "pray[ing] for those who persecute you"? What changes could take place in your heart if you prayed for your adversaries?

7. The author said, "Achieving perfect righteousness is impossible this side of heaven, yet Jesus still calls us to pursue it. And in that pursuit, we pursue God Himself." In what ways are you pursuing righteousness in your life today? What

changes can you make to strengthen your pursuit of God and His righteousness?

Optional Activities

1. Jesus called us to exceed the righteousness of the Pharisees by loving and greeting those outside our family and tribe. Who are some people in your community who may be considered outsiders or even enemies? What can your group do this week to extend love and a gracious welcome to them? Pray together for these "outsiders" and commit to take action to demonstrate God's love to them this week.

2. Break into groups of two or three. Share the name (or initials, for privacy) of someone you know who is hard to love. Pray together for him or her, and ask your group members to help you brainstorm at least one act of grace you can perform for that person this week.

Prayer Focus

Thank God for loving you and sending Jesus Christ to die for you, even when you were His enemy (Rom. 5:8). Confess any bitterness or vengefulness in your heart to Him. Ask Him to help you love your enemies and go the extra mile to share His love with others this week.

Assignment

1. Ask God to bring to mind somebody who has wronged you. Write the person's initials in the space below, and ask God to help you let go of any bitterness toward that person.

2. Read chapter 6 of the *18 Minutes with Jesus* book and work through the corresponding study.

six

Straight Talk about Your Church

SESSION TOPIC: In Matthew 6, Jesus transitioned from how believers are to treat other people to how we are to practice our faith. He began with the practice of giving offerings in church and the attitude behind our giving—whether to please God or to please others. If we seek to please God, then we have a divine reward waiting for us. But if we seek to please others, then we have already received our reward (vv. 1–4).

Icebreakers (Choose One)

1. Choose three or four people in your group to role-play the following situation: a family is getting ready for church on Sunday morning, with typical arguments and frustrations. Then, as soon as they arrive at church, the characters instantly change, smiling and having superspiritual conversation. Discuss: Have you ever experienced something like this on your way to church? Why do you think people tend to put on a "spiritual" face at church?

2. What comes to mind when you think of someone who is a hypocrite? Describe what you think the attitudes and actions of a hypocrite are like in that person's daily life.

Group Discovery Questions

1. Look up *hypocrite* in a dictionary and write what you learn.

2. According to the author, "Hypocrites come in two varieties: those who *knowingly* act a part and deceive others, and those who *unknowingly* act a part and deceive only themselves." Discuss an example of each kind of hypocrite.

3. In what ways can hypocrisy stunt a believer's spiritual growth?

4. Discuss the author's statement: "When unbelievers watch Christian hypocrites, they don't see the attractiveness of the truth; instead, they are repelled by a lie gussied up in religious garb." Do you know any unbelievers who have been "repelled" by hypocrites in the church? How does hypocrisy among believers affect the world's view of Christianity?

5. Read Romans 16:17 and Titus 3:10–11. According to these verses, how should believers deal with hypocrisy in the church?

6. Read Matthew 6:2. What are some current examples of how believers might "toot their own horn" when they do charitable acts?

7. In Matthew 6:3–4, Jesus said when we give to the poor, our giving should be "in secret." Why do you think Jesus commanded us to give anonymous and secret gifts? What blessing did He say a secret giver would receive?

Personal Application Questions

1. Why do you think some believers today pretend to be more spiritual than they really are? Have you ever said or done something to appear more spiritual than you really are? Describe what happened.

2. According to Matthew 15:7–8, which is God more interested in: your outward actions or your heart? Why?

3. Read 1 Corinthians 3:1–3 and Hebrews 5:12–14. On a scale of 1 to 10, with 1 being a spiritual infant needing "spiritual milk" and 10 being a mature Christian able to eat "spiritual meat," how would you describe your level of spiritual maturity right now? What can you do to grow in your spiritual maturity?

4. Read John 12:43 and Galatians 1:10. Whose approval are you seeking in your spiritual life right now? Be honest in your answer.

5. According to Jesus, when people give charitable gifts only to impress others, "they have their reward in full" (Matt. 6:2). What kind of "reward" do they receive? What "reward" do they forfeit (v. 1)?

6. In 2 Corinthians 9:7, the apostle Paul wrote, "God loves a cheerful giver." What do you think it means to be a "cheerful giver"? Have you ever given "cheerfully" to the Lord? If so, describe your experience.

7. Read Acts 20:35. In what ways can a person who gives experience the blessing of God? Consider how you can give selflessly to somebody in need this week.

Optional Activities

1. For Christians, there is no greater joy than investing our time and resources toward making sure people are going to be in heaven. Discuss one way group members can give sacrificially to God's kingdom work this week, such as a collective gift to your church, a group donation to a Christian ministry, or volunteering to serve together at a homeless shelter or missions organization. Discuss any blessings you experience as a result of your gift of time or resources.

2. How would you counsel a new believer on the importance of giving? Share with the group any personal experiences with generosity, whether you obeyed God to give something or you received God's provision through the generosity of others. Read the following verses and discuss what you learn about biblical giving: Proverbs 19:17; Luke 6:38; Acts 20:35; 2 Corinthians 9:6–7; Hebrews 13:16.

Prayer Focus

Thank God for giving you the greatest gift of all—eternal salvation through faith in His Son, Jesus Christ. Confess any hypocrisy or selfish acts you have done to impress other people. Ask God to show you what He would have you do to make the best investment you can make in His kingdom today.

Assignment

1. Examine your personal finances this week. Consider how much you are currently giving to the Lord's work through your tithe to the church and your gifts to other ministries. What changes can you make to increase your giving? Remember, you can't outgive God.

2. Read chapter 7 of the *18 Minutes with Jesus* book and work through the corresponding study.

seven

Straight Talk about Your Prayer Life

SESSION TOPIC: Of all the practices in the Christian life, praying is one of the most fundamental—and one of the most difficult. But it ought not to be. In the Lord's Prayer (which should really be called the Disciples' Prayer), Jesus provided a master class on how to speak to the Father. This prayer's simplicity and straightforwardness are a model for all of us to follow (Matt. 6:5–15).

Icebreakers (Choose One)

1. Who is the first person you contact when you have a prayer request? What do you admire about that person's prayer life? What can you do to follow that person's example in prayer?

2. Have you ever experienced an answer to prayer? Share your experiences with the group.

Group Discovery Questions

1. Why do you think some Christians think prayer is "about as exciting as eating a mashed potato sandwich"?

2. Discuss the author's statement: "My effectiveness in prayer in public is directly correlated to my effectiveness in prayer

in private." Do you agree or disagree? Read Matthew 6:6 to learn what Jesus said about our private prayer times.

3. What did Jesus warn against in Matthew 6:7–8? Do you think God is pleased by lengthy and lofty prayers? Why or why not?

4. Since God already "knows what you need before you ask Him" (Matt. 6:8), why do you think He wants us to pray?

5. Read Matthew 6:9. What is the significance of the phrase "Our Father who is in heaven"? What do you learn about God from this phrase? How can you "hallow" God's name?

6. Read Matthew 6:10. Are you prepared for the day Christ returns and God's kingdom comes? How would our world be different if God's will was done "on earth as it is in heaven"?

7. Read Matthew 6:11–13. Why is it important to ask God for "our daily bread"? How is forgiveness of others linked to God's forgiveness? Why do you think God sometimes allows tests in our lives?

Personal Application Questions

1. Have you ever thought of prayer as "revolutionary"? Why or why not?

2. On a scale of 1 to 10, with 1 being "nonexistent" and 10 being "very strong," how would you describe your prayer life right now?

3. Have you ever been asked to pray in public? If so, what was your response, and why? Why do you think some Christians are afraid to pray in public?

4. Are you taking time in your day for private conversations with the Lord? If so, describe when and where you meet with the Lord daily. If not, choose a place and time to meet with God privately, and then commit to spend time in prayer every day this week. Ask a friend or fellow group member to hold you accountable, if needed.

5. When you pray, do you tend to focus on God first, or do you immediately start asking for your needs? How do you think focusing on God first affects our prayers?

6. Does asking God to meet your daily needs release you from your responsibility to work? Why or why not? Read Deuteronomy 8:18, 2 Thessalonians 3:10, and Colossians 3:23–24, and write out what you learn.

7. Read Matthew 6:12. Who has wronged you and needs your forgiveness? What steps will you take this week to forgive that person?

Optional Activities

1. Break into groups of two or three and pray through the six petitions in the Lord's Prayer:
   - for God's reputation to be honored in your life.
   - for God's justice and mercy to reign in your life.
   - for God's will to be done in your life.
   - for God to take care of your daily needs.
   - for God to forgive you and make you a forgiver.
   - for God to protect you from temptation.

2. Break into groups of two or three. Share a situation in your life you thought of during the lesson. How would praying "Your will be done" (Matt. 6:10) change how you look at the situation? Close in prayer, asking for God's will to be done in your life.

Prayer Focus

Thank God that He desires to communicate with you through prayer. Confess any ways your prayer life might fall short of the way Jesus taught in Matthew 6:5–15. Ask Him to help you deepen your prayer life by seeking Him daily in times of private, simple prayer.

Assignment

1. Start keeping a prayer journal. Write down your requests in a notebook or electronic file, and then record God's answers. Share your answered prayers with the group in future meetings.

2. Read chapter 8 of the *18 Minutes with Jesus* book and work through the corresponding study.

eight

Straight Talk about Your Money

SESSION TOPIC: Wealth (or the lack thereof) and worry go hand in hand, like apple pie and vanilla ice cream. Of all the things that hinder followers of Christ from giving and praying for God's will, perhaps the most crippling is our anxiety over money—worrying whether we have enough or how we can get a little bit more. We desperately need to listen to what Jesus had to say about wealth and put it in its proper place in our lives (Matt. 6:19–34).

Icebreakers (Choose One)

1. Think of a famous person (real or fictional) who was overly concerned with money, such as Ebenezer Scrooge. What caused this person to worry about money? How did this anxiety over money affect the person's life?

2. If you won the lottery tomorrow, what would you do with your winnings?

Group Discovery Questions

1. Discuss the author's statement: "Money and worry are traveling companions. Those who have lots of money worry about losing it; those who have little money worry about getting more of it." Have you or someone you know personally experienced this? Describe the situation.

2. Read Proverbs 23:4–5 and Luke 12:15. What insights do these verses provide about money?

3. Read Matthew 6:19–20. What are some examples of "treasures on earth"? What are some examples of "treasures in heaven"? What can believers do to "store up" heavenly treasures?

4. According to Matthew 6:21, what is "your heart" linked to? How have you seen this link demonstrated in the lives of people you know?

5. In Matthew 6:24, Jesus said, "You cannot serve God and wealth." In what ways do we see people "serving wealth" in our society? Is it possible for a believer to be wealthy without serving wealth? Explain your answer.

6. Read Matthew 6:25–30. How did Jesus tell His followers to respond whenever they were tempted to worry about their needs? What reasoning did He give?

7. According to Matthew 6:31–33, why should Christians' attitude toward money be different from that of unbelievers? What role does our faith play in our perspective of money?

Personal Application Questions

1. On average, how much time in a week do you spend thinking about money or the things money can buy? How much time in a week do you spend thinking about the things of heaven? What can you do to shift your thinking toward heavenly things?

2. Are you content with what God has given you? If not, how much money would it take for you to be content? According to Matthew 6:19, why should you be cautious about storing up "treasures on earth"?

3. Make a list of some things you are worried about right now. How many of your concerns are worries about whether God will meet your needs? What perspective does Jesus's words in Matthew 6:25 provide whenever you are tempted to worry about the things necessary for life?

4. What "treasures" have you stored up in heaven so far? What changes will you make in your life this week to "set your mind on the things above" (Col. 3:2) and "store up . . . treasures in heaven" (Matt. 6:20)?

5. Consider the author's statement: "Jesus said we can either choose God or choose money. We can't choose both—or a percentage of both, a sort of 60/40 split between God and money. The choice we have to make is all or nothing. Both God and money demand single-minded allegiance. . . .

What's it going to be for you—God or money? The choice is yours to make . . . and it has eternal consequences." Where will you choose to place your security?

6. Read Psalm 37:25 and Proverbs 10:3. What do these verses reveal about God's provision for your needs?

7. According to Matthew 6:33, what happens when we choose to make God's kingdom and righteousness our highest priority in life? Write down at least one thing you will do this week to "seek first His kingdom and His righteousness."

Optional Activities

1. Break up into groups of two or three. Share with the group one thing you are concerned about right now, starting with "What if . . . ?" Then ask group members to help you add God to your thinking: "What if . . . ? *But God* . . ." Pray for one another, asking the Lord to help group members trust Him with their cares this week.

2. In Matthew 6:26–30, Jesus used examples in nature to demonstrate God's care. What are other examples of how God provides for His creatures, great and small? If possible, go outside (or look out a window) to observe the many ways God cares for His creation. How can this reminder of God's provision help you when you are tempted to worry?

Prayer Focus

Thank God for His promise to provide all that you need to sustain and enjoy life. Confess any worries you have about money or any ways you have been serving wealth instead of God. Ask the Lord to help you seek first His kingdom and His righteousness in every area of your life.

Assignment

1. What is one thing you have been putting off? Do it this week. If you don't take care of it this week, it will roll over into next week, which only increases your stress and worry.

2. Read chapter 9 of the *18 Minutes with Jesus* book and work through the corresponding study.

nine

Straight Talk about Your Needs

SESSION TOPIC: God created humans to be independent but also *inter*dependent. We are dependent on any number of things to keep us alive and to help us flourish. Simply put, we have needs. And many of those needs cannot be fulfilled by others or within ourselves; only God can fulfill them. But it can be scary relying on God alone, so what did Jesus have to say about that? Plenty. We'll explore what He said in Matthew 7:1–12.

Icebreakers (Choose One)

1. When you were a kid, if someone had given you $1,000 and said you could buy anything you wanted, what would you have bought? What would you spend that money on today?

2. If God promised to grant you one request, what would you ask for?

Group Discovery Questions

1. Discuss the author's statement: "We know we need to do God's will in our lives, but we'd prefer He just rubber-stamp what we want." If God rubber-stamped everything you ever wanted in your life, would you be happy with the result? Why or why not?

2. The popular thinking in our culture today is *We should never judge people*. Read Matthew 7:1–5. Was Jesus saying that we

should never judge anybody for any reason at all? Why or why not?

3. What do you think it means to "take the log out of your own eye" before you help someone else (Matt. 7:5)? Give specific examples of how believers can do this.

4. Read Matthew 7:7–8. Are Jesus's words here a blanket promise that God will give us anything we want if we ask Him? Explain your answer. (Read John 14:13; 15:7 and 1 John 3:22; 5:14–15 to learn some biblical conditions for answered prayer.)

5. According to Matthew 7:9–11, how does your loving heavenly Father respond to your requests when you ask Him in prayer?

6. Why do you think some Christians give up when God doesn't answer their prayers immediately? Read Galatians 6:9, Ephesians 6:18, and 1 Thessalonians 5:17. What do these verses teach us about praying with persistence?

7. Read Matthew 7:12, which is often called the Golden Rule. What are some specific ways believers today can be intentional in living out the Golden Rule in our actions toward others, especially unbelievers?

Personal Application Questions

1. Do you tend to judge other people, even if you don't express those thoughts out loud? How can Jesus's teaching in Matthew 7:1–5 serve as a caution for you whenever you are tempted to judge somebody for doing something you think is sinful?

2. Is there any glaring sin in your life that you haven't dealt with? If so, stop right now to confess that sin to God and ask

Him to remove "the log that is in your own eye" (Matt. 7:3). Thank God for His promise that when we confess our sins to Him, He forgives us (1 John 1:9) and removes our sins from us "as far as the east is from the west" (Ps. 103:12).

3. Have you ever decided not to pray because you thought prayer was unnecessary or unproductive? If so, describe the situation. How do Jesus's words in Matthew 7:7–8 affect your perspective of prayer?

4. If you were absolutely certain that God would hear and answer your prayer, what would you pray for right now?

5. If your child or best friend skinned a knee and asked you for a bandage, would you give that person sandpaper instead? How does your care for a loved one influence your response to a request? How do you think God's love for you influences His response to your requests (Matt. 7:9–11)?

6. Have you ever wanted to pray about something but weren't sure what to say? What encouragement does Romans 8:26–27 give you for those times?

7. How often do you pray for the needs of other people, and not just your own needs? How will you apply the Golden Rule (Matt. 7:12) when it comes to praying for others this week?

Optional Activities

1. On a piece of paper, make a two-column chart with one column labeled "My Needs" and the other labeled "My Wants." Under "My Needs," list things you genuinely need in life. Under "My Wants," list things you would like to have but are not necessary for survival. What perspective do you gain on your life from this exercise?

2. Break into groups of two or three and give a blank note card to each person. Ask each group member to share one prayer

request, and write all the requests on your notecard. Close in prayer, then put the notecard in your Bible or somewhere you will remember it. Commit to pray persistently for these requests every day next week, and then follow up about these requests in your next group meeting.

Prayer Focus

Thank God for being a good heavenly Father who meets all your needs. Confess to Him if you have a "log in your eye"—any sin in your life that you haven't yet dealt with. Ask Him to help you treat others the way you want to be treated and to make your attitudes and actions reflect Jesus Christ.

Assignment

1. Memorize Matthew 7:7–8: "Ask, and it will be given to you; seek, and you will find; knock, and it will be opened to you. For everyone who asks receives, and he who seeks finds, and to him who knocks it will be opened."

2. Read chapter 10 of the *18 Minutes with Jesus* book and work through the corresponding study.

ten

Straight Talk about Your Eternal Destiny

SESSION TOPIC: One of the greatest fears people have is of the future. Is there really a heaven and a hell? And if there is, how can we be sure where we'll spend eternity? We'll see how Jesus answered these questions in Matthew 7:13–27. His answers are just as applicable today as they were two thousand years ago.

Icebreakers (Choose One)

1. We all make choices in life—some are insignificant, while others have lasting effects. Describe one significant decision you've made, such as which college to attend, what career to pursue, where to live, or whether to marry or have children. How has that decision influenced your life?

2. Why do you think our society rejects the idea that there's only one path to heaven?

Group Discovery Questions

1. According to Matthew 25:46, what are the two possible destinations when we die?

2. Read Matthew 7:13–14. What destination does the "broad" path lead to? What destination does the "narrow" path lead to? According to Jesus, how many people find the "narrow" gate?

3. How did Jesus describe Himself in John 14:6? What do you learn from this verse about how to get to heaven?

4. What did Jesus say about "false prophets" in Matthew 7:15? What kinds of things do false prophets say today, especially when it comes to the gospel?

5. According to Matthew 7:16–20, how can we identify false prophets? What is an example of "bad fruit"? In contrast, what would "good fruit" look like?

6. Read Matthew 7:21–23 and discuss the author's statement: "To me, those are some of the most terrifying words in the New Testament. Jesus was saying that on the broad path that leads to hell are many people who claim to be Christians. Hell won't just be populated with unrepentant murderers, rapists, and drug dealers but also with religious people, even people who have deceived themselves into thinking they are Christians." According to verse 21, what characterizes true Christians?

7. In Matthew 7:24–27, Jesus contrasted those who only hear His instructions with those who hear *and obey* His instructions. Since the Bible is clear that salvation is by faith in Jesus Christ (Eph. 2:8–9), what is the role of obedience in the Christian life? (For more insight, read James 1:22; 2:14–20.)

Personal Application Questions

1. Read Deuteronomy 30:19, Joshua 24:15, and Jeremiah 21:8. What do you learn from these verses about the two eternal destinations and our responsibility to choose?

2. According to James 4:14 and 2 Corinthians 6:2, why is it essential for you to be sure of your eternal destination *today*?

3. Read Matthew 7:20. What kinds of "fruits" are in your life right now? What do these "fruits" reveal about your salvation?

4. In Matthew 7:21, Jesus said, "He who does the will of My Father who is in heaven will enter" the kingdom of heaven. Have you done "the will of My Father" by placing your faith in Jesus Christ for salvation? Read Romans 10:9–10 and Acts 4:12; 16:30–31, and write what you learn about how to be saved.

5. According to Matthew 7:22–23, Jesus knows what's going on inside the hearts of those who call Him Lord. Read 1 Samuel 16:7. When the Lord looks at your heart and weighs your motives, what do you think He sees? What changes, if any, would you like to make?

6. According to Matthew 7:24–27, how can you tell whether something has a strong foundation? Think of a "storm" that came into your life. What did that storm reveal about the nature of your faith? What can you do to strengthen your spiritual foundation so that when you face storms in the future, your faith will stand firm? Be specific.

7. Consider the author's statement: "Only one kind of person is a true follower: the one whose faith in Jesus Christ is proved through obedience to His Word. Only one kind of person can have the assurance of eternal life: the one whose faith in Jesus Christ can withstand the judgment of God." According to this description, are you a true follower of Jesus Christ? Explain your answer. If not, see the prayer in Optional Activity #2 below.

Optional Activities

1. Break into groups of two or three, and do the following role-play: A person is having dinner with a friend, and the friend says, "I think people can believe whatever they want to believe and live however they want to live, and everything will turn out okay in the end." How would you respond to him or her? Use Scripture to support your answer.

2. Where do you want to spend eternity? There is only one path to heaven, and that narrow path is only through faith in Jesus Christ. Have you come to Christ in faith and sought His forgiveness for your sins? If not, God's forgiveness is available to you right now! If you desire to receive God's forgiveness and know for sure that one day you will be welcomed into heaven, then you can say a prayer that goes something like this, knowing that God is listening:

Dear God, thank You for loving me. I know I have failed You in so many ways, and I'm truly sorry for the sin in my life. I believe that You love me so much You sent Your Son, Jesus, to die on the cross for me and take the punishment I deserve for my sins. And right now, God, I am trusting in what Jesus did for me, not in my good works, to save me from my sins. Thank You for forgiving me, and help me to live the rest of my life for You. In Jesus's name I pray, amen.

Prayer Focus

Thank God for the many insights and challenges He has brought to you through this study. Ask Him to help you answer His call to radical righteousness and live life differently.

ABOUT DR. ROBERT JEFFRESS

Dr. Jeffress is senior pastor of the fourteen-thousand-member First Baptist Church, Dallas, Texas, and is a Fox News contributor. He is also an adjunct professor at Dallas Theological Seminary. Dr. Jeffress has made more than two thousand guest appearances on various radio and television programs and regularly appears on major mainstream media outlets, such as Fox News Channel's *Fox and Friends, Hannity, Fox News @ Night with Shannon Bream*, and *Justice with Judge Jeanine*, as well as ABC's *Good Morning America* and HBO's *Real Time with Bill Maher*.

Dr. Jeffress hosts a daily radio program, *Pathway to Victory*, that is heard nationwide on over one thousand stations in major markets such as Dallas–Fort Worth, New York City, Chicago, Los Angeles, Houston, Washington, DC, Philadelphia, San Francisco, Portland, and Seattle.

Dr. Jeffress also hosts a daily television program, *Pathway to Victory*, that can be seen Monday through Friday on the Trinity Broadcasting Network (TBN) and every Sunday on TBN, Daystar, and the TCT Network. *Pathway to Victory* also airs seven days a week on the Hillsong Channel. His television broadcast reaches 195 countries and is on 11,295 cable and satellite systems throughout the world.

Dr. Jeffress is the author of twenty-seven books, including *Perfect Ending, Not All Roads Lead to Heaven, A Place Called Heaven, Choosing the Extraordinary Life, Courageous, Praying for America,* and *Invincible.*

Dr. Jeffress recently led the congregation of First Baptist Dallas in the completion of a $135 million re-creation of its downtown campus. The project is the largest in modern church history and serves as a "spiritual oasis" covering six blocks of downtown Dallas.

Dr. Jeffress holds a DMin from Southwestern Baptist Theological Seminary, a ThM from Dallas Theological Seminary, and a BS degree from Baylor University. In May 2010, he was awarded a Doctor of Divinity degree from Dallas Baptist University. In June 2011, Dr. Jeffress received the Distinguished Alumnus of the Year award from Southwestern Baptist Theological Seminary.

Dr. Jeffress and his wife, Amy, have two daughters and three grandchildren.

ABOUT *PATHWAY TO VICTORY*

Established in 1996, *Pathway to Victory* serves as the broadcast ministry of Dr. Robert Jeffress and First Baptist Church of Dallas, Texas.

Pathway to Victory stands for truth and exists to pierce the darkness with the light of God's Word through the most effective media available, including television, radio, print, and digital media.

Through *Pathway to Victory*, Dr. Jeffress spreads the good news of Jesus Christ to lost and hurting people, confronts an ungodly culture with God's truth, and equips the saints to apply Scripture to their everyday lives. More than a thousand radio stations in the United States broadcast the daily radio program, while Daystar, Trinity Broadcasting Network, and other Christian television networks air *Pathway to Victory* both in the United States and internationally.

Our mission is to provide practical application of God's Word to everyday life through clear, biblical teaching. Our goal is to lead people to become obedient and reproducing disciples of Jesus Christ, as He commanded in Matthew 28:18–20. As our ministry continues to expand, we are confident the Lord will use *Pathway to Victory* to advance the mission statement of First Baptist Dallas: to transform the world with God's Word . . . one life at a time.